THE EUGÉNIE ROCHEROLLE SERIES

Intermediate Piano Solo

Valses Sentimentales

7 Original Solos by Eugénie Rocherolle

To Peggy Otwell

2   Bal Masqué (Masked Ball)

6   Jardin de Thé (Tea Garden)

10   Le Long du Boulevard (Along the Boulevard)

28   Marché aux Fleurs (Flower Market)

14   Nuit sans Étoiles (Night Without Stars)

18   Palais Royale (Royal Palace)

24   Promenade à Deux (Strolling Together)

PLAYBACK+
Speed • Pitch • Balance • Loop

To access audio, visit:
www.halleonard.com/mylibrary

Enter Code
2674-9944-8884-1151

ISBN 978-1-4234-3563-1

Visit Hal Leonard Online at
www.halleonard.com

World headquarters, contact:
Hal Leonard
7777 West Bluemound Road
Milwaukee, WI 53213
Email: info@halleonard.com

In Europe, contact:
Hal Leonard Europe Limited
42 Wigmore Street
Marylebone, London, W1U 2RY
Email: info@halleonardeurope.com

In Australia, contact:
Hal Leonard Australia Pty. Ltd.
4 Lentara Court
Cheltenham, Victoria, 3192 Australia
Email: info@halleonard.com.au

BAL MASQUÉ
(Masked Ball)

By EUGÉNIE ROCHEROLLE

Allegro (♩ = 152)

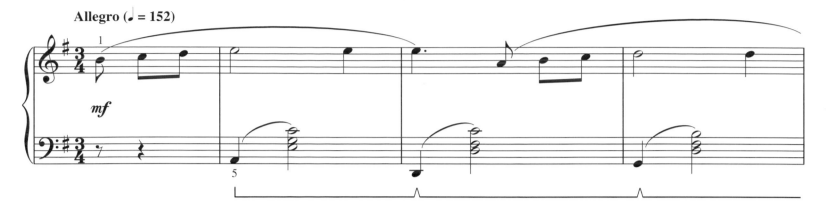

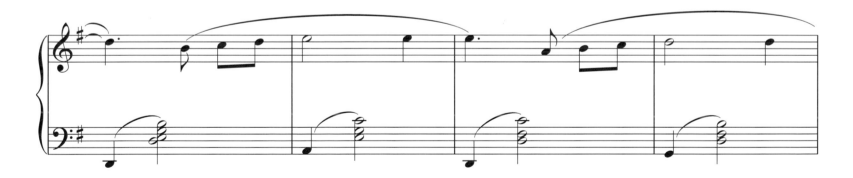

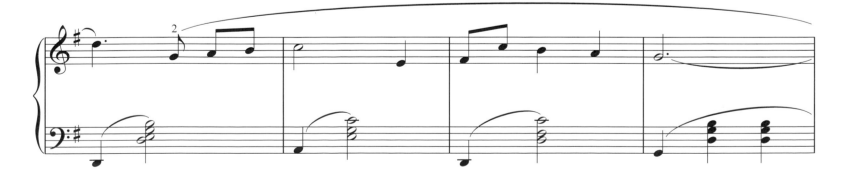

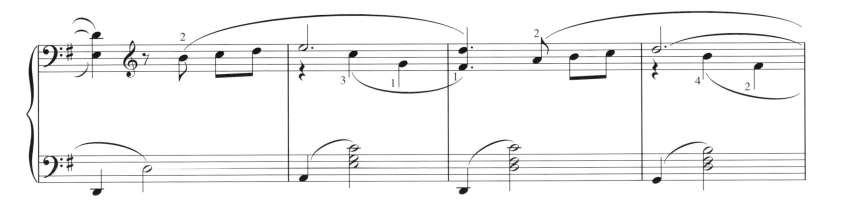

simile

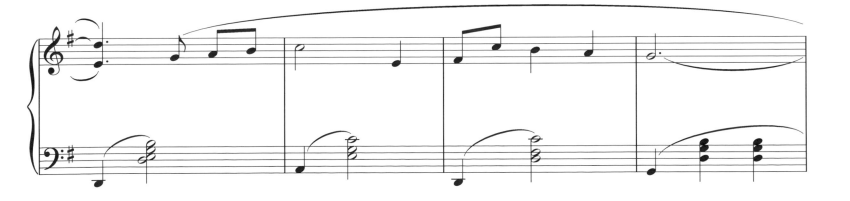

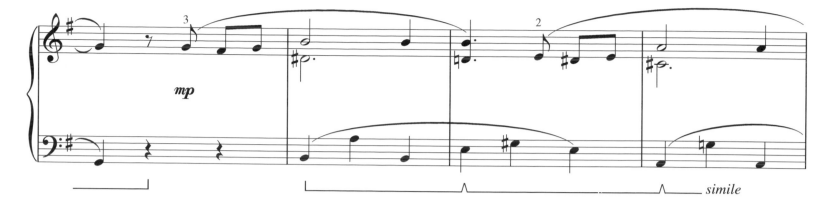

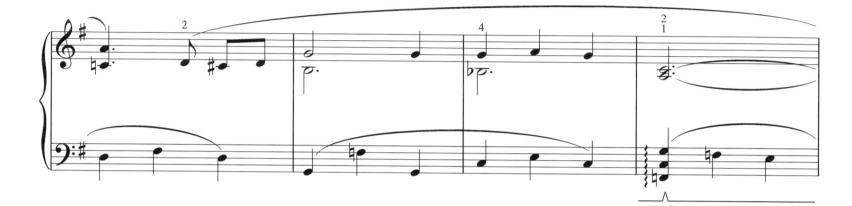

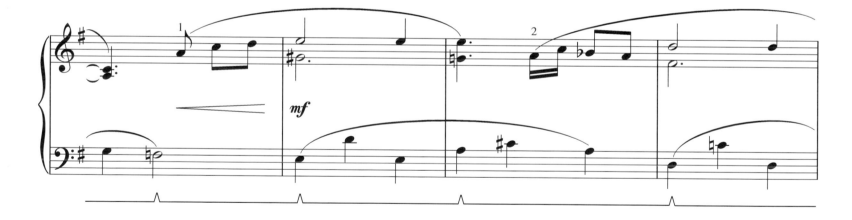

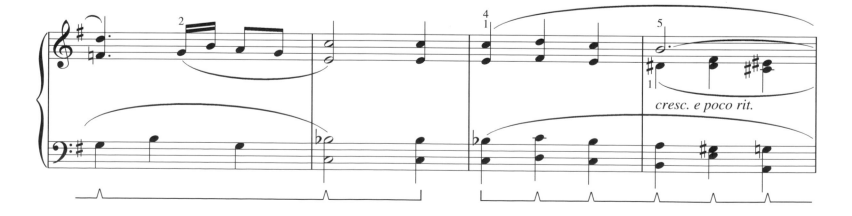

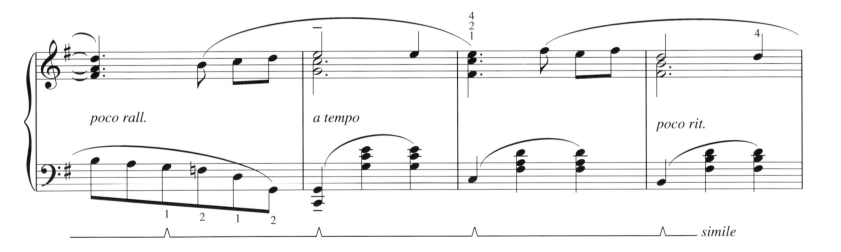

JARDIN DE THÉ
(Tea Garden)

By EUGÉNIE ROCHEROLLE

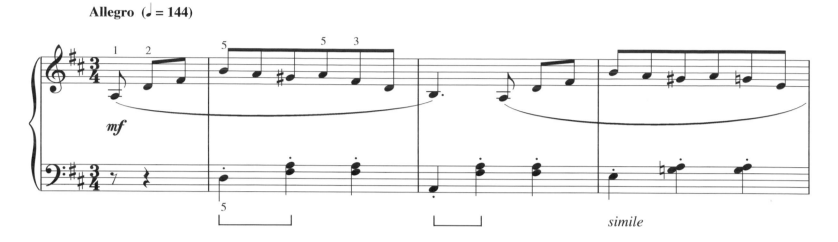

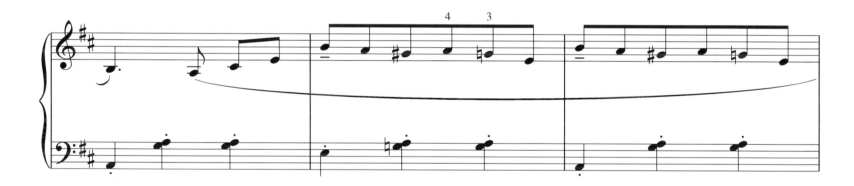

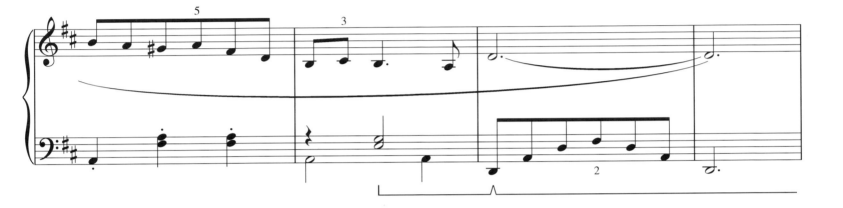

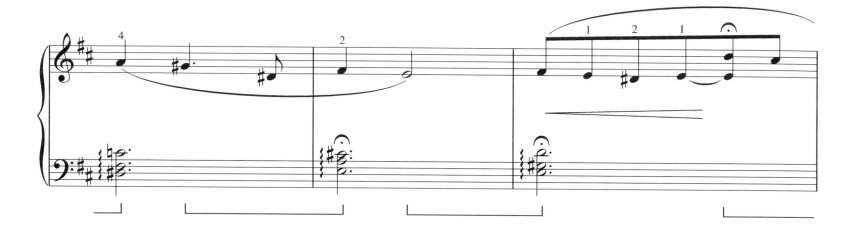

9

LE LONG DU BOULEVARD
(Along the Boulevard)

By EUGÉNIE ROCHEROLLE

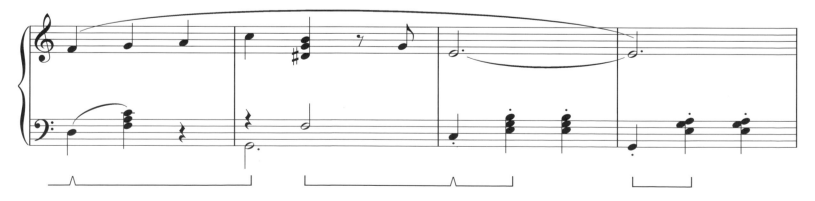

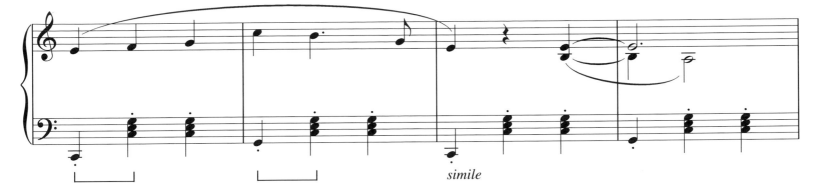

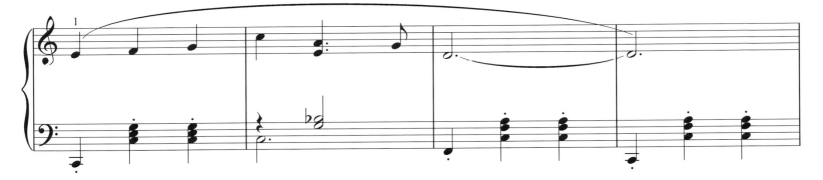

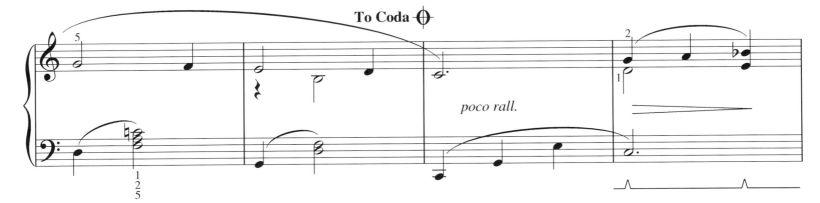

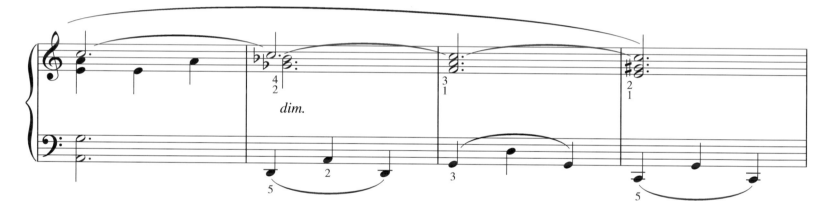

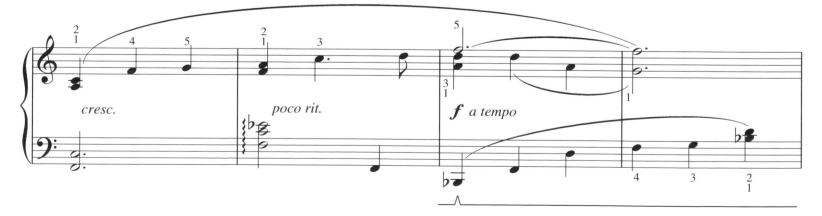

mf

simile

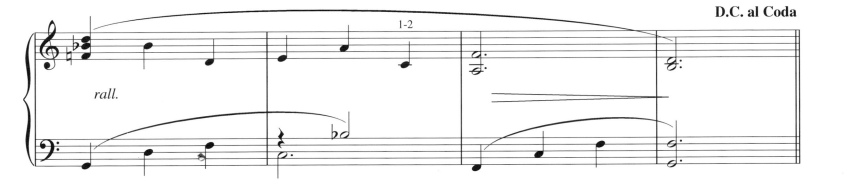

D.C. al Coda

rall.

1-2

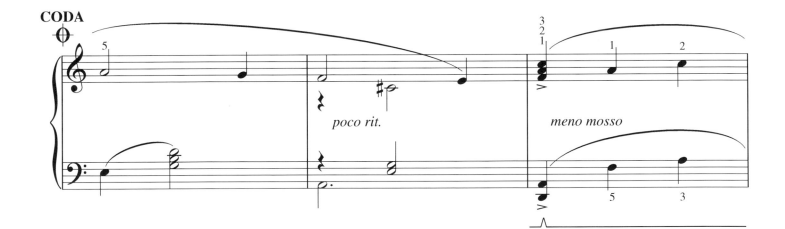

CODA

poco rit.

meno mosso

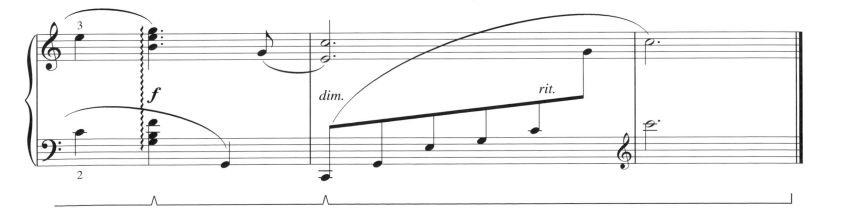

f

dim.

rit.

NUIT SANS ÉTOILES
(Night Without Stars)

By EUGÉNIE ROCHEROLLE

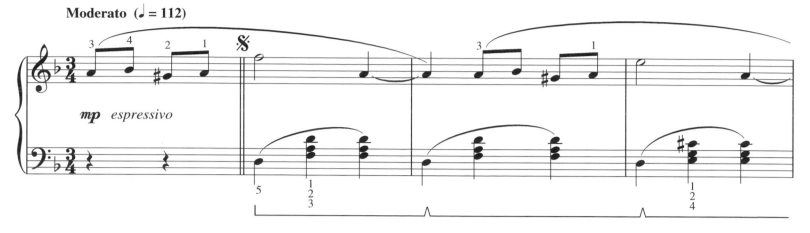

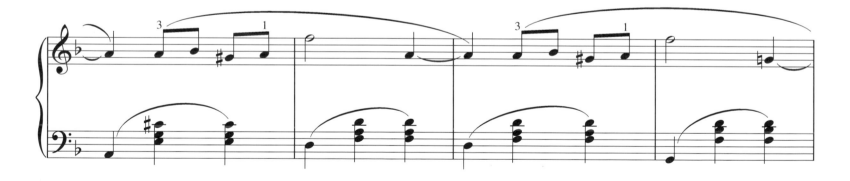

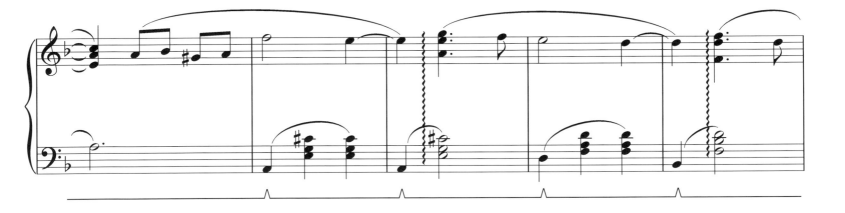

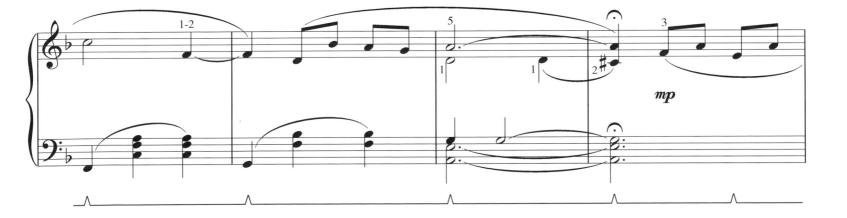

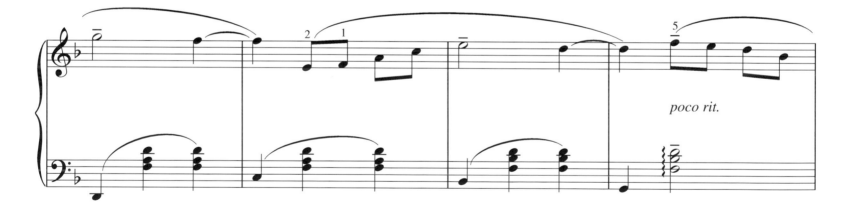

CODA

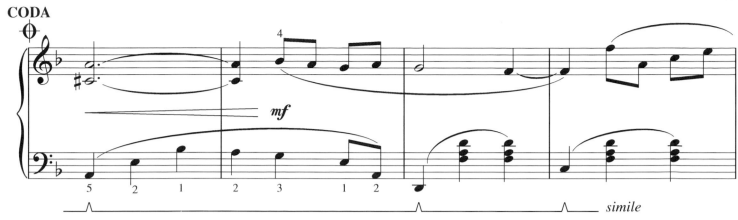

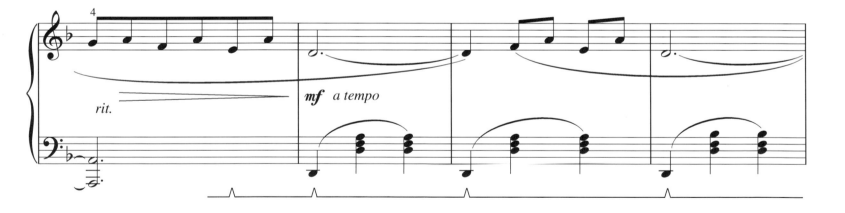

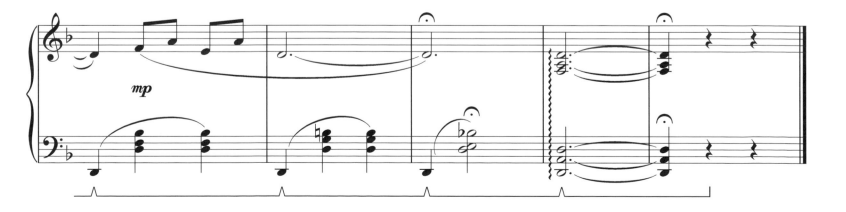

PALAIS ROYALE
(Royal Palace)

By EUGÉNIE ROCHEROLLE

Molto allegro (♩. = 63)

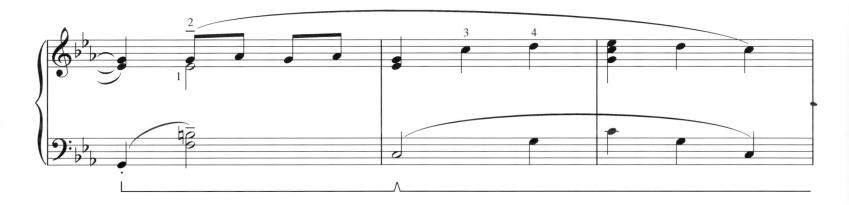

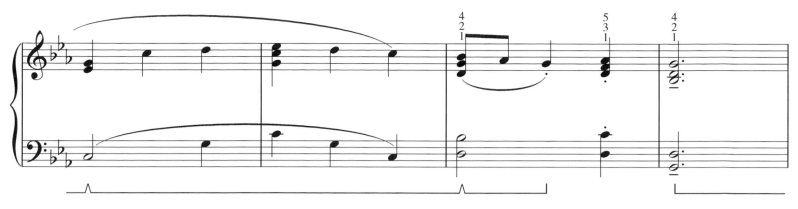

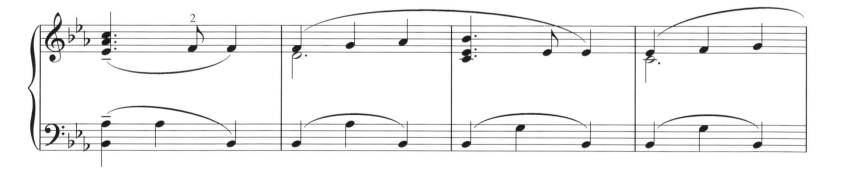

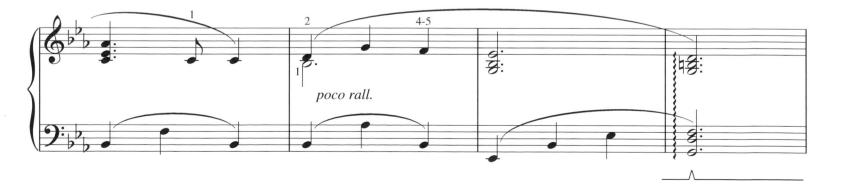

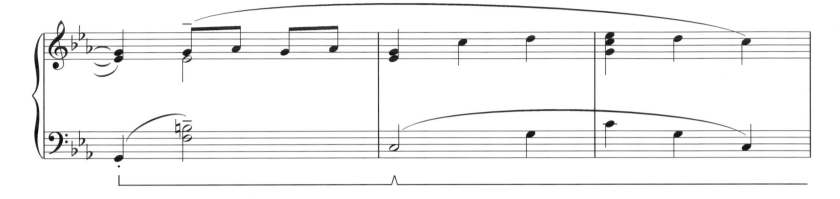

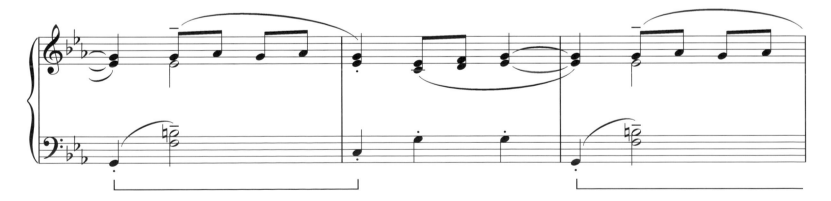

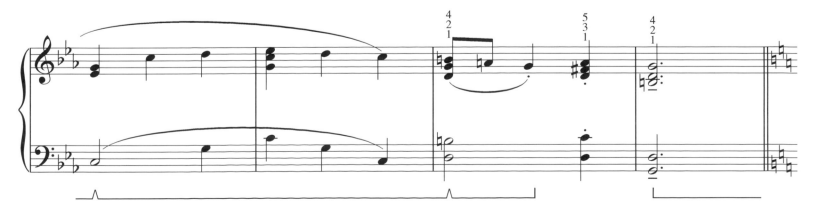

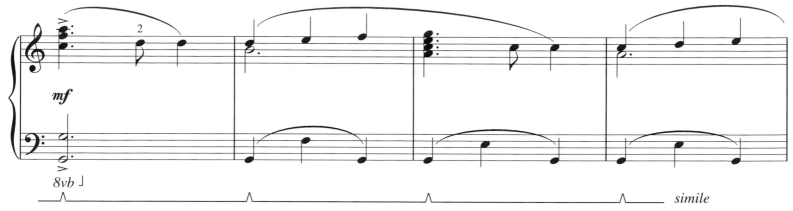

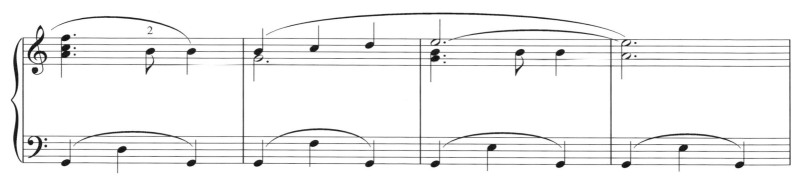

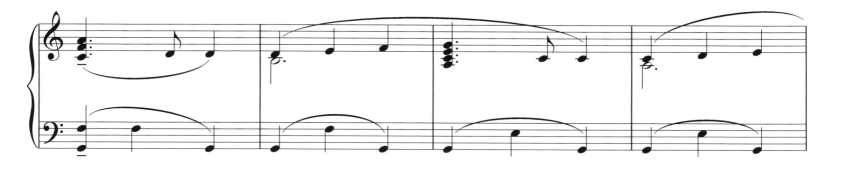

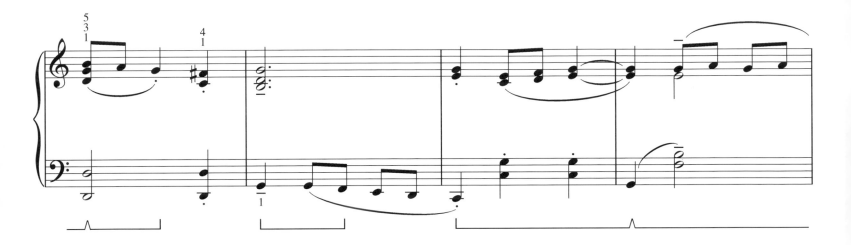

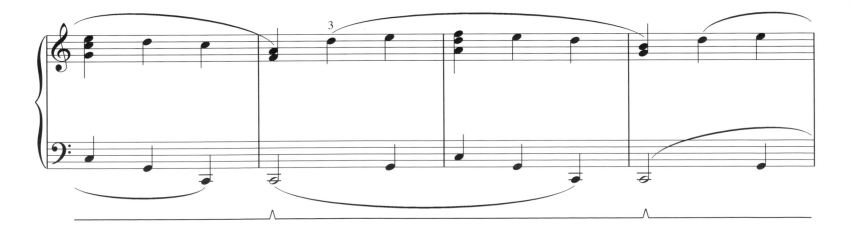

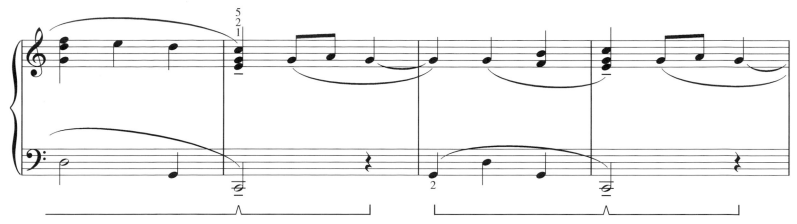

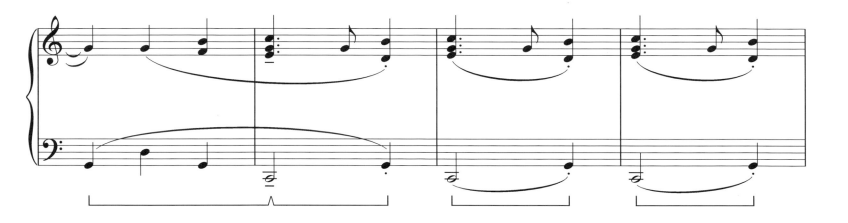

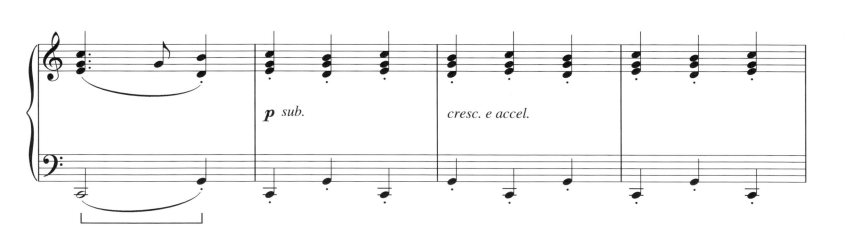

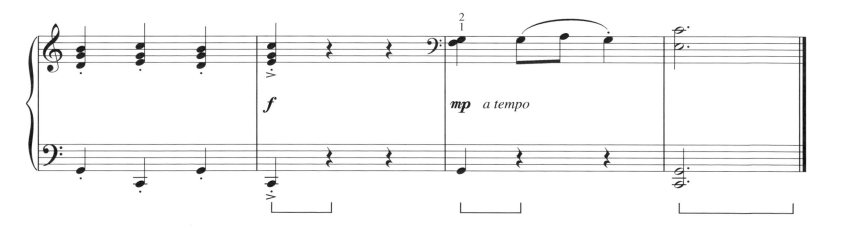

PROMENADE À DEUX
(Strolling Together)

By EUGÉNIE ROCHEROLLE

Allegro (♩ = 132)

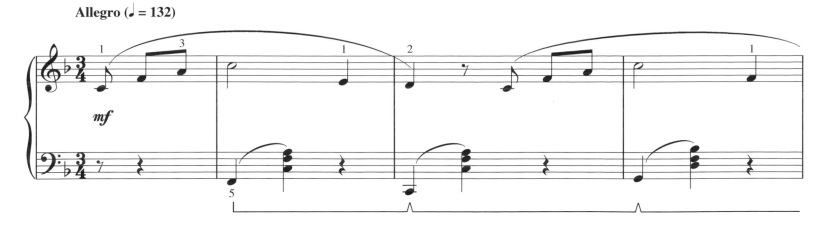

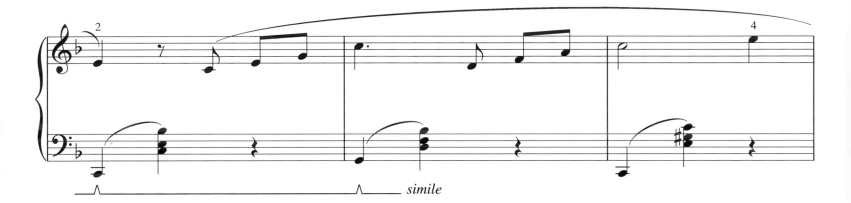

simile

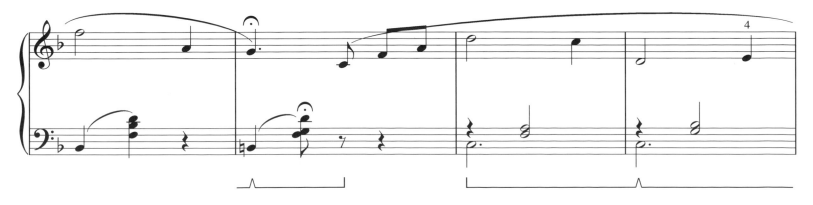

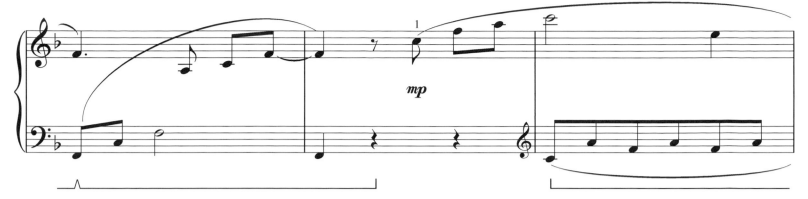

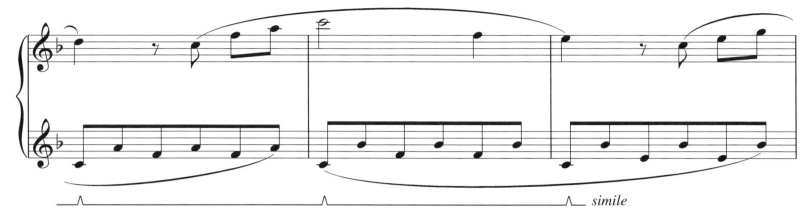

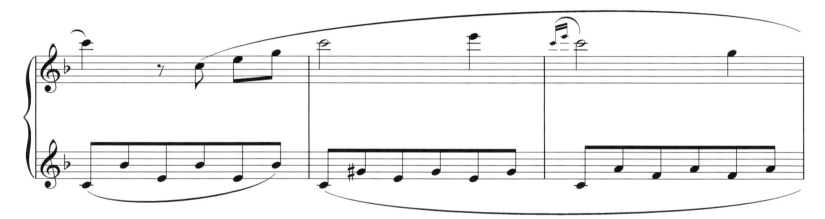

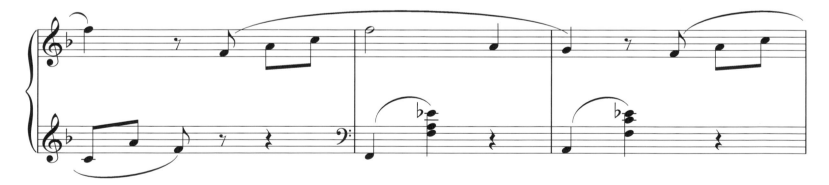

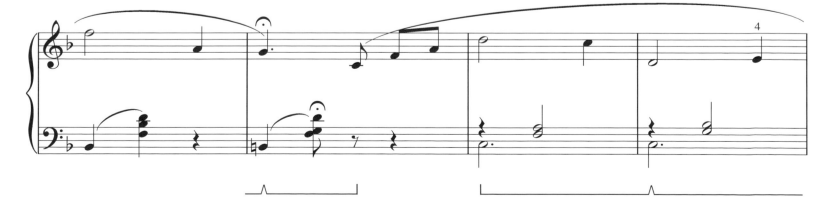

Poco mosso

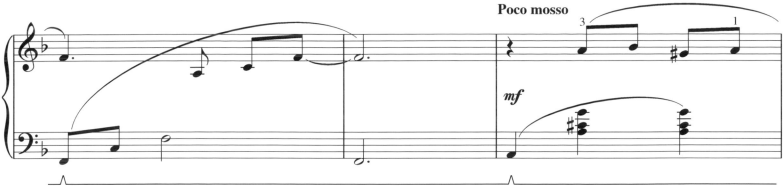

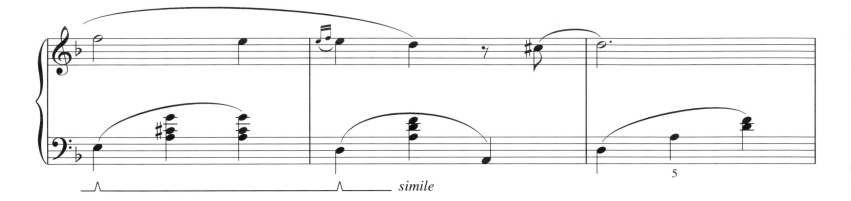

simile

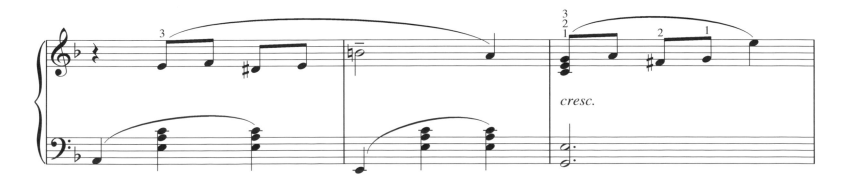

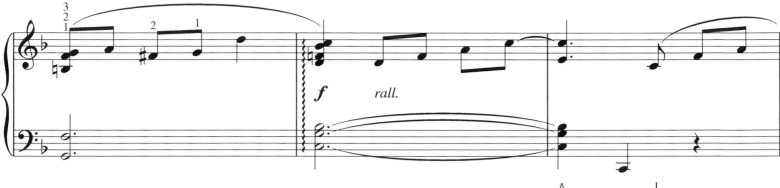

Tempo I

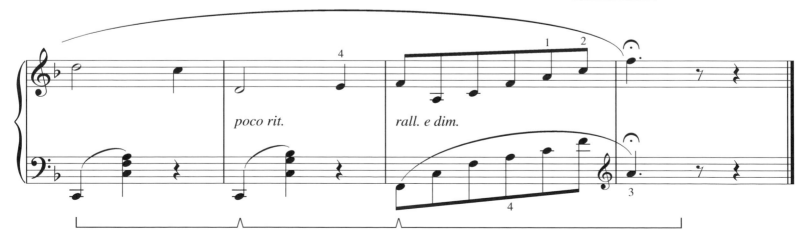

MARCHÉ AUX FLEURS
(Flower Market)

By EUGÉNIE ROCHEROLLE

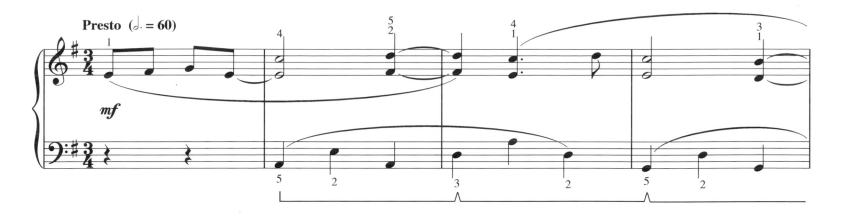

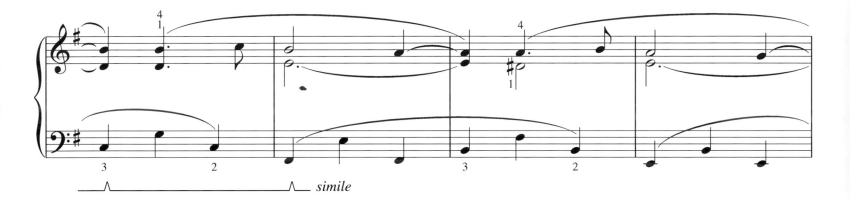

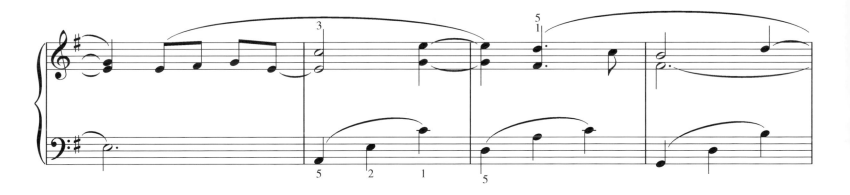

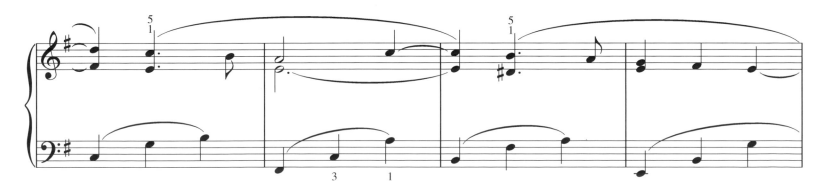

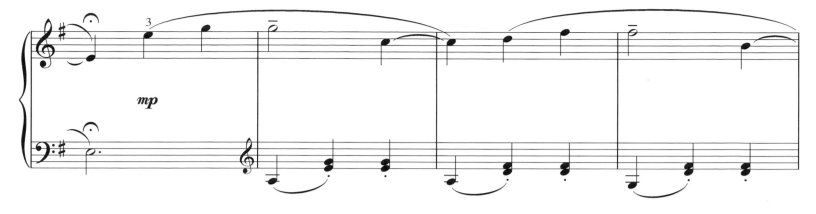

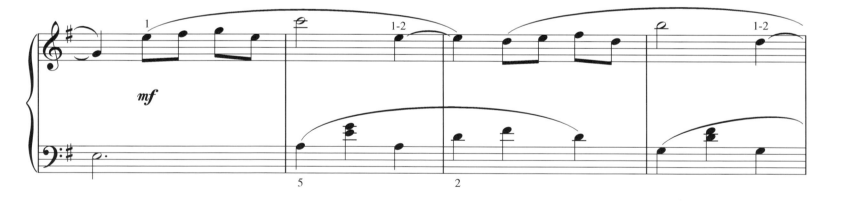

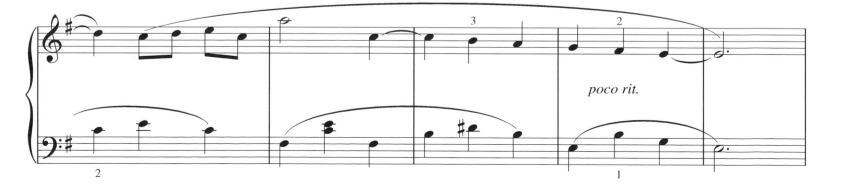

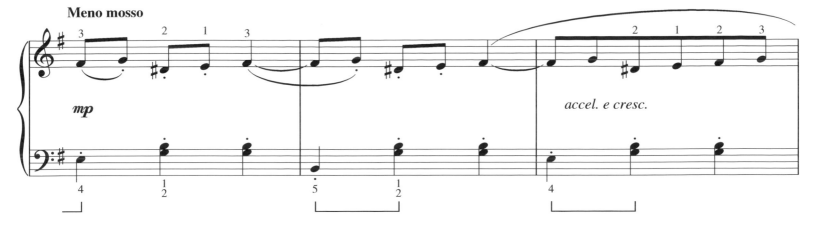

Meno mosso

mp

accel. e cresc.

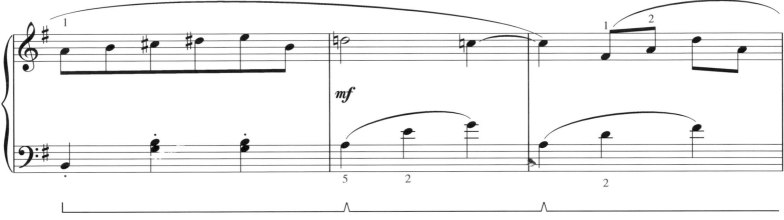

Tempo I

mf

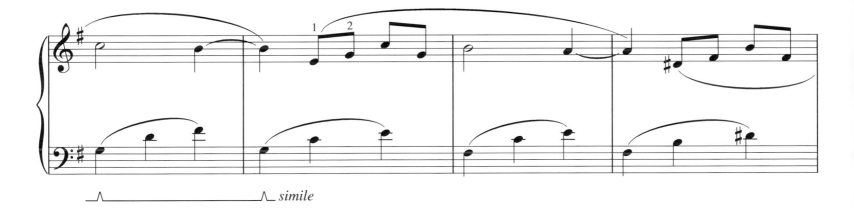

simile

Meno mosso

mp

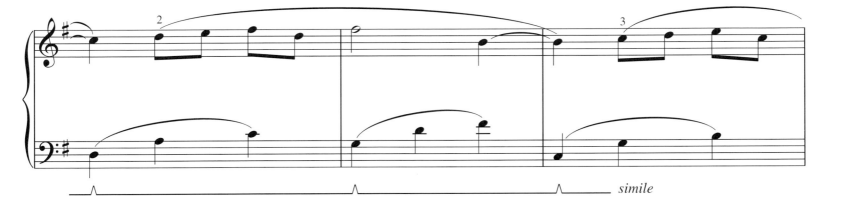

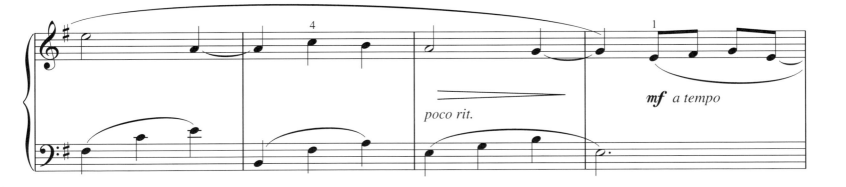

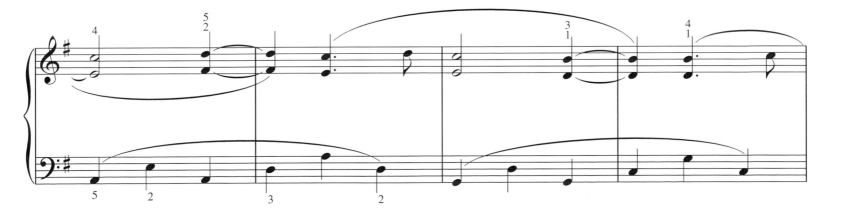

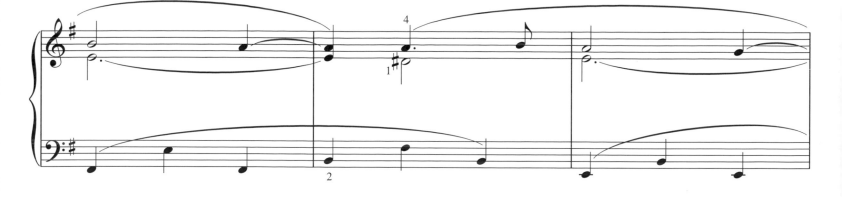

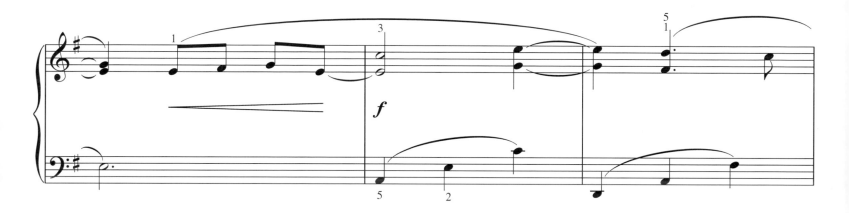

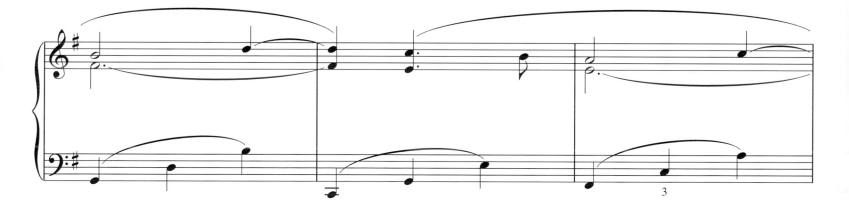

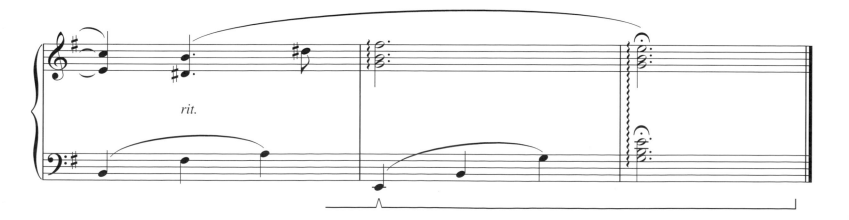